CAREERS IN CRIMINAL JUSTICE™

CAREERS IN THE CORRECTIONS SYSTEM

DANIEL E. HARMON

ROSEN PUBLISHING®

New York

Published in 2010 by The Rosen Publishing Group, Inc.
29 East 21st Street, New York, NY 10010

Copyright © 2010 by The Rosen Publishing Group, Inc.

First Edition

Library of Congress Cataloging-in-Publication Data

Harmon, Daniel E.
Careers in the corrections system / Daniel E. Harmon.—1st ed.
    p. cm.—(Careers in criminal justice)
Includes bibliographical references and index.
ISBN-13: 978-1-4358-5266-2 (library binding)
1. Corrections—Vocational guidance—United States.
2. Vocational guidance. 3. Job hunting—United States.
I. Title.
HV9471.H34 2010
365'.973023—dc22

                                                    2008040845

Manufactured in China

CONTENTS

INTRODUCTION

Most people who pursue careers in law enforcement are interested in preventing crimes, solving mysteries, catching criminals, or bringing wrongdoers to justice. In the corrections system, the crimes already have been solved and the criminals already have been caught, tried, and sentenced. The main task of a corrections professional is to help administer the punishment process securely, humanely, effectively, and with a view toward someday returning the criminal to a productive life in society. It's a rewarding career path—but one with unavoidable risks.

Young people who are interested in corrections careers should be encouraged by hiring statistics. Qualified corrections professionals are in increasing demand for the simple, sad reason that more and more people are violating laws and are being placed under correctional supervision. Many states are imposing longer sentences for the most serious crimes. This has the effect of slowing the prisoner release rate while the intake rate continues to increase. Newspaper reports and television documentaries frequently describe dangerous

Corrections workers at any facility are a diverse team with different characteristics, skills, and educational and experience levels. These professionals serve in various roles at the Franklin Correctional Institution in Florida.

overcrowding in jails and prisons throughout the United States. New facilities are constantly being built to house rising inmate populations. Additional trained staff members are needed to operate them.

Surveys made by the Bureau of Justice Statistics, part of the U.S. Department of Justice, show that by December 31, 2006, 7.2 million adults were under correctional supervision in the United States. That meant 3.2 percent of the U.S. population, or one in thirty-one adults, was an offender within the corrections system. The 2006 total was an increase of about 160,000 offenders over the 2005 statistics.

Of the number of supervised offenders at the end of 2006, about five million were living in the community, on probation or parole. The others were housed in prisons, jails, or other detention facilities, or were being supervised at halfway houses and in alternative punishment programs.

As the offender population increases, so must the staff at correctional facilities. Not all corrections officers are prison guards. Counseling and supervisory employees work constantly with both inmates and those who have been released on probation or parole. Needed professionals include specialists who have management, clerical, psychological, medical, and other forms of training. Every job category calls for dedicated employees who possess a combination of the right skills, education, talents, interests, and attitude to make an effective corrections officer.

If a corrections worker performs with dedication, job security is practically assured. However, many workers in time decide to abandon their careers. Turnover is common because the job—especially for corrections officers who are in daily contact with dangerous criminals—can be highly stressful.

Although the growing number of convicted offenders is disturbing and staff burnout often occurs, aspiring corrections workers can be excited about the opportunities for them to make a positive impact. Regardless of their job titles, if they perform well, corrections workers contribute to a better society. Because of what they do, lives that have gone astray can be changed dramatically.

CORRECTIONS IS A *BIG* SYSTEM

The Fourteenth Amendment to the U.S. Constitution says no state may deprive anyone of life, liberty, or property "without due process of law." State and federal laws stipulate that if a person is duly convicted of a crime, as punishment the individual may lose one or more of those fundamental privileges—even life, in extreme cases. The corrections system was created to carry out the punitive responsibility of government.

The corrections system overall is not the same thing as the prison system. It includes the prison system, but it is much more than a society of prisoners living behind bars and fences. Corrections is the complex system under which persons convicted of crimes undergo not merely punishment but rehabilitation and, in many cases, treatment. In some states, extraordinary murder cases—execution-style mass murders, serial killings, the slaying of law enforcement officers, exceptionally savage acts, and the murder of children—may bring the death penalty (deprivation of life). Many types of convictions call for imprisonment (loss of liberty). Other sentences include fines, forfeiture, and/or restitution (loss of property).

But the objectives of today's corrections system aren't just to protect society from convicted lawbreakers. Corrections professionals also try to help return offenders to meaningful, productive places in society. That dual mission—protecting the public while transforming misguided individuals—calls for career-minded individuals who have a unique desire to contribute to a better community.

A GUILTY VERDICT DOES NOT ALWAYS LEAD TO PRISON

When people are convicted of wrongdoing, they do not all go through the same correctional processes. The sentencing judge may commit them to one of many different programs or facilities. For the simplest misdemeanors—speeding violations or possession of marijuana, for example—there may be hardly any correctional process at all beyond, perhaps, a lecture from the judge. The guilty person might be ordered to pay a light fine or may be dismissed with simply a warning. A vandal might be ordered to pay restitution for property that was

damaged or lost. An accessory to a crime might be penalized by forfeiture—being forced to give up certain property that was used in an illegal act (an automobile or weapon, for instance).

State laws specify the appropriate range of punishment for different crimes. Laws vary from state to state. For example, there are two kinds of larceny (theft), which are defined by the value of the stolen property. Grand larceny, involving higher

Some prisons are small and house only a few hundred inmates. Others are sprawling complexes that require hundreds or even thousands of staff members. This aerial view shows California State Prison, Corcoran.

values, is a felony that can result in imprisonment. Petit (petty, or minor) theft is a misdemeanor that might be dismissed with a fine and/or probation. The dividing line, in terms of stolen property value, is not the same in every state. The same amount of stolen goods can land a culprit in prison in one state but bring only a rap on the knuckles in another. Meanwhile, the highest form of punishment—the death penalty—is allowed in thirty-seven states but is shunned in the others, where life imprisonment without parole is the maximum sentence.

If more than an immediate fine or payment of restitution is called for, the guilty party enters a segment of the corrections system. Not all forms of correction require confinement, but they all impose accountability. At the least, they require the wrongdoer to demonstrate an understanding of the error and an intention to go straight.

Non-confinement components of the system are twofold: probation and parole.

Probation means the person can go free immediately after conviction—under certain conditions. The judge typically announces a jail or prison sentence (or a hefty fine), but in the same order reduces the sentence to probation (a brief period of incarceration, followed by a longer term of probation). The guilty person who is willing to meet the terms of probation can avoid the formidable fine or confinement. But if during the probationary period the person violates the court order, the court may reinstate the original, heavier sentence.

What are the terms of probation? The person must regularly meet with a probation officer and answer questions about any personal activities from day to day, including events at work or during recreational times. If the subject is found to be lying or commits another crime while on probation,

A probation officer investigates an offender's background in Franklin County, Florida. Probation and parole officers are two of the many types of professionals who are vital to the nation's correctional system.

freedom may be taken away. Depending on the crime, other conditions may be imposed. If the person completes the probationary period without incident, the correctional process is completed.

Judges are most likely to reduce a sentence to probation for first-time offenders and youthful offenders. The reasoning is that if a violator's wrongdoing results from an impulsive, thoughtless act or from immaturity, the community is better served in the long run by giving the person another chance. Incarceration not only can cast the first-time offender among hardened felons, it will also cost the state a significant amount of money to keep the individual confined.

Probation is granted immediately after a person's conviction, during the sentencing phase. Parole, by contrast, applies at the further end of the correctional process. It is a shortening of the sentence after a prisoner has served a portion of it.

In many criminal cases, a sentencing judge issues an indeterminate sentence—not a specified number of months or years, but a *time frame*—during which justice can be satisfied. An indeterminate sentence might specify "two to six years" of incarceration. The decision of exactly how long the inmate will serve is left to the parole board of that jurisdiction. The board periodically reviews the prisoner's records and interviews the prisoner, as well as individuals who may have an impact on an early release decision. In many cases, if the inmate has a record of good behavior while serving time, the board will grant a parole. The prisoner is released before the maximum sentence is carried out but remains accountable to a parole officer. The released inmate must report regularly, much like the person on probation. Depending on conditions of the parole, the inmate might, for example, be forbidden to leave the state during the parole period. If the parolee is convicted of another

Leslie Van Houten (*right*), a member of the infamous Charles Manson "family," appeared at a parole hearing in 2002 in California. Van Houten, convicted in a 1969 murder case, was denied parole.

crime during the parole period, the original sentence will be reinstated, in addition to sentencing for the new offense.

Both probation and parole processes require specially trained professionals within the corrections system. They must manage their cases carefully and determine whether the individual is truly fit to be free in the community. In some cases, they recommend that probation or parole be reversed.

From Simple to Complicated Arrangements

Small town and county American jails have always struggled on shoestring budgets. Until recent years, simplicity and practicality were the essential operating principles.

The Lexington County (South Carolina) Jail as recently as the 1960s was an aging, two-story brick building staffed by a single jailer. The county sheriff's family lived upstairs, and the sheriff's wife served as cook for the prisoners. Town drunks and other petty offenders actually looked forward to periodic incarceration. Although roaches and rats sometimes joined them, and heating and cooling were primitive in their cells, they knew they would receive three square meals and a bath. That situation was not unlike those at many other jails across the United States in bygone days.

The modern-day Lexington County Detention Center that replaced the old jail in 1975 is a state-of-the-art compound that has been expanding ever since it was built. At present, it can temporarily house almost a thousand inmates in three buildings. Ninety professionals—security, administrative, and supervisory workers—operate the center. Obviously, career opportunities at this one correctional facility alone have multiplied rapidly.

Prisons and some local jails today are much larger. Some require several hundred staff personnel to supervise five thousand or more inmates.

LIFE BEHIND BARS AND RAZOR WIRE

The main objective of a facility of incarceration is to keep convicted criminals away from society at large. But while doing that, the prison or detention center must provide proper housing and care for inmates. It must see that their basic human rights are not violated.

Jails are short-term places of confinement. They are not designed to house an inmate for longer than a few days, weeks, or months. The inmate capacities of most jails is no more than a hundred, although some jails are larger and, at times, are forced to house a thousand or more prisoners.

Many jail inmates are people who have been arrested and charged with a crime and are awaiting their day in court. Others have been tried and con-victed, or pleaded guilty, and have been sentenced to short periods of confinement. Convicted felons who have been sentenced to longer prison terms are sometimes held temporarily in jails until correctional authorities can find them a permanent place.

Prisons, operated by state or federal governments, are intended to house felons who must serve longer sentences. Not all prisons are alike. Different facilities are designed to accommodate different types of criminals. Maximum-security prisons house those who are considered the most dangerous. Inside them, some inmates, because of dangerously violent personalities or the nature of the crimes they committed, are kept apart from the general prison population.

One institution especially noted for its infamous residents is California State Prison, Corcoran. Inmates in its Protective Housing Unit include Charles Manson, who directed his cult "family" to carry out multiple, gruesome murders in 1969. Another resident of the unit is Juan Corona, convicted of murdering twenty-five itinerant farm workers in 1971.

At the highest security level—"super-maximum" prisons or "control units"—extremely dangerous criminals are kept in solitary confinement most of the day. When they are released from their cells, they are shackled.

Minimum-security institutions house those who have committed less serious crimes and who are not considered dangerous to society. In some minimum-security environments, prisoners enjoy certain freedoms and comforts inside the prison and may even be allowed weekend visits outside.

Between maximum and minimum security are different levels of severity. Special detention facilities house juvenile inmates and certain types of law-breakers who require special treatment, such as disabled or substance-dependent individuals. Near the end of their sentences, many prisoners are allowed to complete their terms in halfway houses. These are supervised homes within the community

Convicted of murder and conspiracy along with other members of his "family" of followers in 1971, Charles Manson was originally sentenced to death. He is now serving a life sentence at California State Prison, Corcoran.

where inmates can gradually adjust to reentry into society.

In some cases, convicted individuals may not have to serve inside institutions alongside more serious offenders, but they may lose some of their freedoms. They might be confined to their homes under the custody of relatives, for example, or they might have to wear electronic monitoring devices. Their sentence may consist of reporting for community service work each weekend for a period of time.

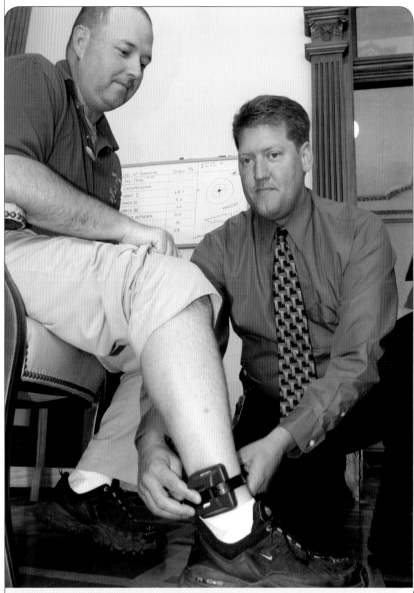

These probation officers in Troy, Ohio, demonstrate an ankle monitor that can reveal whether or not a person on probation has been drinking. The device analyzes the wearer's sweat.

Home confinement is not just for petty or first-time offenders, but it is also used as a step toward a longtime prisoner's reentry into the community. The Federal Bureau of Prisons frequently places inmates on home confinement as they approach the end of their terms (within the final six months or 10 percent of their sentence periods). During this prerelease time, most prisoners are expected to find jobs and are required to remain at home when they are not working. The objective of the program, the bureau explains, is to provide "an opportunity for inmates to assume increasing levels of responsibility, while, at the same time, providing sufficient restrictions to promote community safety and convey the sanctioning value of the sentence."

In each situation, specially trained workers are needed to oversee the correctional process.

EMERGING ISSUES THAT AFFECT THE CORRECTIONS JOB MARKET

Some states, mainly in the West and South, have contracted with private management firms. These organizations build and operate correctional institutions (mostly minimum and medium security) for the government. They often build module-like buildings, which are less expensive to construct than buildings with unique designs. They provide

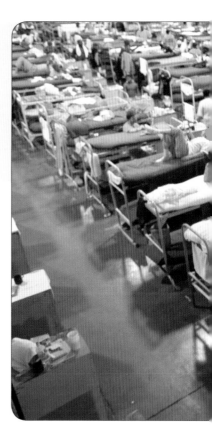

Overcrowding forced officials to fill San Quentin's prison gymnasium with bunk beds. Confinement in such close quarters unavoidably results in tension and violence among inmates and dangers for corrections staff.

an additional, though comparatively small, job market for people interested in corrections careers.

This concept of "privatization" in corrections (critics call it "prisons for profit") has brought protests from some quarters. At the heart of the concern is that constitutionally, only the state has the authority to prosecute, convict, and punish lawbreakers. It is not authorized to delegate punishment to a private contractor. Skeptics also point out that if a prison is run by a private corporation,

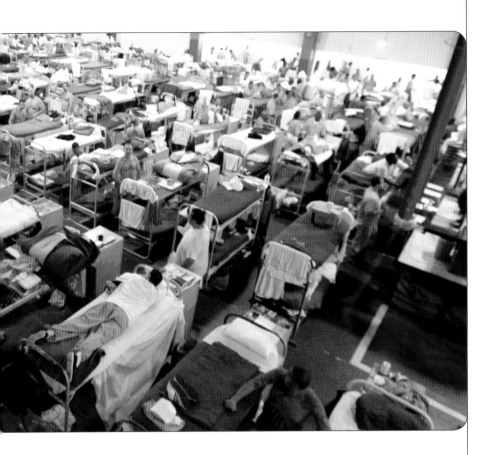

it's in the corporation's best interest to keep the facility at full capacity at all times. And they worry that private operators are less likely than government employees to uphold inmates' rights.

Such legal and ethical questions regarding privatization are fairly recent and are only one small part of broader concerns voiced by watchdogs of the entire corrections system. Greater issues involve inhumanity, mainly a result of overcrowding, and basic human rights. Besides losing their freedom, convicted criminals forfeit certain rights under law. However, they are not "slaves of the state," as an 1871 court ruling, *Ruffin v. Commonwealth*, once branded them. The number of lawsuits brought by inmates against prison guards and administrators has increased dramatically in recent years. The suits—many of them brought by prisoners who have studied the law—range from charges of negligence (ignoring symptoms of illness, for instance) to unnecessary brutality.

Besides the punishment requirement, prisons are expected to provide treatment for inmates who suffer from illnesses or addictions, and rehabilitation for all those who are expected to return to society. Still, jails and prisons are not fun places to be. Most cells are stark, with only the most essential furnishings. (One reason for bare cells is that angry inmates sometimes try to destroy anything they can get their hands on.) Many prisoners may be crowded into a single, small jail cell. Even in situations where well-behaved inmates are allowed to possess certain amenities—TV sets, personal libraries, mini-refrigerators—confinement is punish-ment indeed.

Across the nation, maintaining such a large and complex system of corrections calls for professionals who have many types of training and experience. Many young people are interested in the security

Different Systems, Different Employment Needs

Missouri, a state in the center of the country, had just more than 100,000 criminal offenders in its corrections system in June 2008. About two-thirds were on probation or parole. Almost 30,000 were institutionalized. Besides more than 700 community release centers, Missouri operates 270 residential facilities, twenty of which are adult correctional centers.

The Missouri Department of Corrections (DOC) employs about 12,000 workers at more than ninety sites throughout the state. As in other states, the growing number of offenders results in a growing corrections job market. The Missouri DOC states in its Web site's human resources section, "That creates a constant, critical need to recruit and retain a dynamic workforce. Qualified professionals looking for a challenging career should take a serious look at the Missouri Department of Corrections." It adds, "Our team is making a difference every day."

California operates thirty-three adult correctional facilities, fifteen institutions and community-based camps for juveniles, thirteen community correctional facilities, and—interestingly— forty-six conservation camps for adult and juvenile offenders. The latter institutions, called "fire camps," engage minimum-security offenders in fighting wildfires—a ceaseless problem in California. These individuals, who save state taxpayers an estimated $80 million per year, obviously require supervisors with unique training.

aspect of corrections as a career. Others who envision careers in education, medicine, psychology, management, and other fields may not realize that those careers are part of corrections systems. They may discover that corrections is the most rewarding scenario in which to pursue their dreams.

PRISON AND JAIL SECURITY— WHERE OFFICER MEETS INMATE

Corrections officers—guards and security workers—are the point professionals in the corrections system. They are the ones who must monitor inmates and ensure control over every interaction that takes place among prisoners, and between prisoners and outside individuals who enter the facility. Their tasks include preventing escapes, fights among residents, and illegal activities within the jail or prison population; overseeing inmate work projects; regularly inspecting cell blocks and other areas of the compound; and periodically searching prisoners and cells for contraband. They also perform less dramatic chores— writing reports and inspecting the facility to make sure it is constantly sanitary and free of safety hazards. Day after day, their jobs might seem routine, at times boring. But without warning, a crisis can arise. They know it would be foolish to forget the dangers.

Officers participate in a ten-week training course on inmate discipline procedures. After their initial training, corrections professionals must take classes from time to time on emerging topics and issues involving jail and prison systems.

Known as corrections officers at prisons, these professionals may be called jailers or detention officers at local and county jails and detention centers. At each type of facility, the duties and expectations of the corrections officer call for special individuals who have been well prepared. Approximately half a million people were employed as corrections workers in the United States as of 2006, according to the *Occupational*

Outlook Handbook. About 300,000 of them worked in state-run institutions.

AN ATMOSPHERE OF TENSION

No jail or prison is a relaxing place to live or work. Many prisoners are noisy and aggressive. TVs and radios blare throughout the cell blocks. Most facilities are overcrowded. California State Prison, Corcoran, for example, houses some 2,500 more prisoners than its official capacity of 3,100. Many prisons are outdated—poorly ventilated and poorly lit, with frequent plumbing and structural problems. Tempers flare easily among inmates.

Because of this, corrections officers are always on guard. They must be especially alert when inmates are together in common areas—dining halls, showers, and exercise grounds. Even when the surroundings seem calm, corrections professionals know the inmates are living under duress. This tension extends to the prison work staff. Guards must always be mindful of what is going on among prisoners, watching for signs of danger. They come to know prisoners' individual traits. They are aware of the subcultures that exist within the inmate population—the gangs, the group leaders, the potential troublemakers, and the coded signals gang members use to communicate.

New Castle Correctional Facility was the scene of an inmate riot in 2007. The violence erupted over a clothing issue and resulted in injuries to several staff members and inmates.

Most prisoners who enter the corrections system just want to serve their sentences and return to free society as soon as possible. They are not trouble-makers by nature. But other inmates are violent and domineering by nature. This results in a very com-plex social structure within the prison population. It produces power struggles and clashes among racial and special-interest factions. Corrections officers are required to maintain control. Sometimes, they have to use force to keep order.

A racial conflict apparently sparked a riot at a
Los Angeles County, California, prison in 2006.
One inmate died and more than one hundred others
suffered injuries ranging from slight to serious.
Prisoners elsewhere have reacted violently to matters
as seemingly trivial as clothing. An incident of this
kind occurred at a privately operated prison in
New Castle, Indiana, in 2007. Inmates from Arizona,
unhappy with their relocation to the Indiana prison,
refused to wear issued clothing at lunchtime. When

Attica and Other Prison Uprisings

The nation was stunned in September 1971 when prisoners at the maximum-security Attica State Correctional Facility in New York State conspired to capture some thirty guards and commandeer a cell block. Holding the guards hostage, the prisoners demanded more than two dozen reforms, from more acceptable meals to expanded religious freedom. Prison officials agreed to many of the demands but refused on one key point: to grant amnesty to the rebellious inmates. After four days of negotiations, law enforcement officers stormed and recaptured the cell block. Thirty-two prisoners and eleven guards were killed.

Attica is the most infamous of modern-day prison revolts, but they continue. In New Mexico in 1980, inmates seized control of an entire penitentiary for a day and a half. They held twelve guards hostage. Although the guards eventually were released, thirty-three prisoners were killed and the premises were ransacked. Most of the victims were executed by other inmates who suspected them of being informers.

A 1989 riot at a Pennsylvania institution resulted in the destruction of almost half the prison property and more than one hundred injuries. Altercations involving fewer inmates and negligible damage and injuries, although not widely publicized, are common throughout the country. They remind corrections staff that potential dangers in such settings are never far away.

members of the corrections staff confronted them, they responded violently. A corrections supervisor was beaten, and seven inmates and two guards received minor injuries.

It may seem surprising that in many correctional settings, officers are unarmed when they're in direct contact with prisoners. One reason for this is to avoid the risk of losing their weapons in the event of a group attack. However, their movements are under perpetual surveillance, and outside colleagues are ready to assist quickly should trouble occur.

A select few corrections professionals are specially trained for tactical response teams, also called special reaction teams. These units deal with riots, hostage crises, the forced removal of inmates from cells or other areas, and other dangerous situations. Besides advanced training in weapons (including the use of tear gas and rubber bullets and grenades) and self-defense, they must have knowledge of potential threats such as poisons and other chemical agents.

MUCH MORE THAN "GUARDS"

A corrections officer at any institution—federal or state prison, city or county jail, or special facility for youthful offenders or those with psychiatric or substance abuse problems—must perform multiple tasks. It is by no means a matter of simply carrying a gun and monitoring inmates' behavior. The duties of corrections officers might include the following:

- Conducting frequent head counts among prisoners
- Ensuring exterior gate and interior door security
- Inspecting the facility—especially entrances, windows, and locks
- Serving as guards and tower sentries (sentries, armed with rifles, are selected for their superior marksmanship)
- Receiving and processing incoming prisoners, including fingerprinting or photographing the offenders for record files
- Labeling and storing new arrivals' belongings that are not allowed inside a cell

Some corrections officers are trained investigators who can probe crimes that are committed inside the prison. Transportation officers bring new inmates into the compound and are trained to securely transport prisoners who are scheduled for court appearances or parole hearings, or who require hospitalization outside the prison. Other officers constantly monitor inmates via surveillance cameras. Prisoners are under watchful eye while

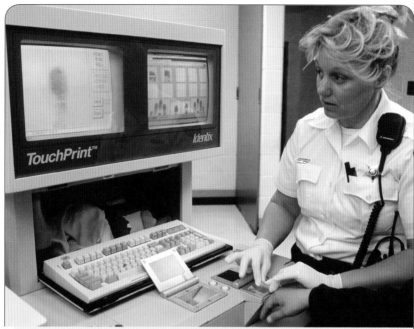

With computer technology, this jail booking officer can process fingerprints quickly and accurately. The system uses digital images instead of ink and enters the print records into a national fingerprint database.

they are eating, exercising, lounging, bathing, working—and even sleeping.

And there are routine duties: keeping daily records of prisoner activities, monitoring and distributing mail to inmates, providing them with toiletries and other necessities, monitoring visitation, and accompanying inmates to educational classes and work assignments inside the institution.

At some county and municipal jails, jailers are not career corrections officers but are new deputies or police officers who are assigned to guard duty. This specified task gives them experience with the criminal element within a controlled setting before they are sent out on patrol. During this period, some law enforcement rookies decide they want to devote their careers to corrections, rather than to public police duty.

FEDERAL, STATE, OR LOCAL?

Corrections officers are needed at every kind of facility, and those needs are growing. Although job tasks may be similar at each level of government facility—federal, state, and local—the required education and experience are not the same. Nor are the pay scales or the prospects for promotion.

At the federal level, corrections officers are needed not just inside federal prisons but at other agencies. The U.S. Immigration and Naturalization Service employs a trained corrections staff, including armed officials who must temporarily detain people suspected of citizenship violations. The Bureau of Indian Affairs also needs corrections workers. Even the National Park Service (NPS) must sometimes detain, process, and counsel individuals who are arrested at park sites. Most NPS corrections personnel—like those in other agencies that are not primarily concerned with detention and correction—are law enforcement officers who can also perform correctional duties, as needed.

Corrections specialists work in the military branches, which are part of the federal government. The U.S. Marshals Service (under the Department of Justice) also needs corrections professionals to house, transport, and oversee prisoners who have been arrested by the FBI and other federal law enforcement agencies. U.S. marshals are responsible for the accused individuals' security until their day in court.

The daily tasks of corrections officers in federal institutions are much the same as those of workers in state prisons. However, prisoners convicted of federal crimes are, for the most part, considered especially threatening to society.

Federal corrections jobs pay more than those at state and local facilities. Not surprisingly, they have greater requirements. Whereas many state and municipal institutions require only a high school diploma for applicants to entry-level positions, federal jobs are more likely to call for either a four-year degree or a combination of college credits and experience. Most federal jobs also require special security clearance, which entails more stringent testing and background checks of applicants than those for state or local positions.

A fugitive turns himself in to a U.S. marshal in Akron, Ohio. A new program of the U.S. Marshals Service allows fugitives to surrender without confrontation.

STRESS AND INCONVENIENCE COME WITH THE JOB

The best corrections officers treat prisoners with respect and even with a degree of friendliness. They win respect from some of the inmates in return. They provide job information and advice that can help offenders readjust to society after their releases. These are some of the personal services they can provide, and the later testimonies of offenders who benefited from their help are the foremost rewards of their jobs.

But officers know they can never become too friendly with prisoners. They know where to draw the line between friend and guard. They understand how the criminal mind works and how people in confinement are masters of manipulation. And they know that many of the prisoners they oversee, although they might appear friendly on the surface, hate them simply because corrections officers represent authority.

Aspiring corrections officers should consider other worrisome aspects of the job before proceeding into this career path, including the following:

Corrections officers typically work eight-hour shifts—and the shifts change. The officer will work regular daytime hours for a while, then rotate to evening hours, then to early morning hours.

Expect to share weekend and holiday obligations with colleagues. Correctional facilities never close, and supervision must be constant. Every employee takes part in the 24/7/365 regimen.

Many correctional facilities are in rural, isolated locations. That means many employees face the annoyance and expense of long commutes to and from work.

ORDER IN THE COURT

Some corrections-related security tasks are performed outside prisons and jails. In courthouses (all levels of criminal court), bailiffs are the officers responsible for keeping order and ensuring the protection of everyone in the courtroom. They escort juries between the courtroom and the deliberation chamber, to lunch, and—in lengthy trials—to and from court-arranged lodgings. They scan people entering the courtroom for weapons and keep a watchful eye for suspicious behavior during hearings and trials. They silence or oust talkers. Two or more bailiffs usually serve together.

Bailiffs are officers of the court. But in most situations, they are paid by a related law enforcement agency. The U.S. Marshal Service oversees federal court bailiffs. State or circuit court bailiffs are provided by the sheriff's department of the county in which the courthouse is located. Municipal court bailiffs are paid by the city or town police department. A detachment of armed law enforcement officers almost always is present to assist bailiffs when criminal court is in session.

Since courts are not constantly in session, many bailiffs are hired part-time. Others are full-time law enforcement personnel assigned temporarily to serve a court as corrections officers.

Besides maintaining order when court is in session, the bailiff is responsible for overseeing courtroom maintenance. This includes every detail, from electrical systems and lighting to sanitation. Bailiffs also run errands for judges, other court officials, and jury members.

New Opportunities for Women

Until the mid-1900s, almost all corrections officers were men. They were taught not to let prisoners or parolees "get out of line." To make sure they kept control, they did not hesitate to use physical force, sometimes brutally.

Women have been part of prison systems for centuries, but their roles have been limited. In times past, they were hired only to perform clerical work (typing or record keeping), nursing, and classroom instruction. Some were responsible for keeping the guards' arsenal of weapons in top condition. The few who were armed and trained as

Millicent Newton-Embry became one of the nation's first African American female wardens in 2004. She was appointed warden of Mabel Bassett Correctional Center in McLoud, Oklahoma.

guards were assigned to surveillance towers, away from immediate prisoner contact in the grounds and cell blocks.

Men and women of different races make up today's security staffs inside prisons and detention centers. A court ruling in 1982 forbade discrimination against women applicants for all corrections roles. At about the same time, the rising percentage of female prisoners in the United States began to climb significantly. More than 112,000 women were in confinement at the end of 2006, according to the Bureau of Justice Statistics. Women corrections officers at all levels have found a growing demand for their services. Some have risen to the top corrections career position: prison warden.

ADVANCEMENT POTENTIAL

What are corrections officers' prospects for career advancement?

Corrections sergeants oversee a facility's security staff and earn higher salaries. A few officers ultimately become wardens or deputy wardens. Many more, though, discover that other jobs within the corrections system interest them especially. Workers with prison security experience obviously bring a special understanding into later jobs as counselors or parole officers. Some leave the corrections system to pursue other types of criminal justice jobs—particularly police work. In order to make a career adjustment, they may need to obtain further education and training.

The job of corrections officer is only one of many career avenues in this field. Possibilities for meaningful corrections-related employment are almost unlimited.

3

VARIED CAREER OPPORTUNITIES IN CORRECTIONS

Jailer. Guard. Caseworker. Social worker. Substance abuse counselor. Job trainer. Chaplain. Legal professional. Response team weapons and tactics specialist. Clerical worker and records keeper. Administrator. Cook. Parole officer. Doctor and licensed therapist. Halfway house director. Community work project supervisor. Psychologist. Budget preparer. Prison design architect. Public information director. Deputy warden. Warden.

The corrections officers described in the previous chapter are the personnel most people think of when they consider the role of "corrections professionals"—the guards with the guns. But it takes many more people with many diverse talents and training to maintain a secure and effective correctional facility. It takes many more people to return lawbreakers to productive lives in society, and to help ensure that they don't reenter the corrections system.

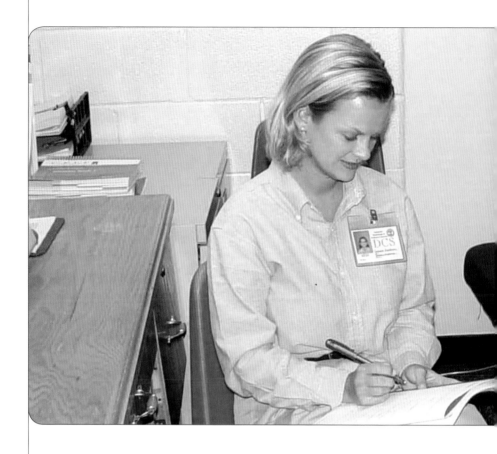

Because of this, the corrections system is a wide open career field. The Federal Bureau of Prisons, for example, employs more than four thousand psychologists. It also offers advanced careers in such areas as corrections program planning and training.

PROBATION AND PAROLE OFFICERS

Most convicted criminals in the United States are not incarcerated. They are either out on probation

Psychologists and psychiatrists are among the professionals with advanced education who choose to establish their careers inside correctional institutions. They help inmates who have emotional or mental problems.

or out on parole. That means the courts and corrections authorities deem them to be safe members of ordinary society—but they must follow specified rules of conduct and report regularly to their probation or parole officers. More than ninety thousand probation officers are at work in federal, state, and local corrections systems, according to the Bureau of Labor Statistics. The number of available jobs in probation may increase by as much as 20 percent by 2012, according to the bureau. The job market for parole officers is more limited.

Probation and parole officers need skills that are not required of other corrections professionals. They must be a combination supervisor, counselor, investigator, effective communicator, careful observer, and paper shuffler. They must have computer skills and be able to write thorough, clear reports on their clients' progress during the supervisory period. They are a bit like police officers, but more like social workers.

Probation officers are assigned by the court to supervise offenders with suspended sentences. But beforehand, they may be called on to investigate the case and the offender's background prior to sentencing and to advise the court as to an appropriate sentence. They check the criminal and employment histories of the convicted person, talk to victims, and talk to arresting officers. They interview relatives, medical or counseling professionals, and others who may have insight about the individual. The information they glean can affect the nature and severity of the sentence. In some instances, the probation officer concludes that the offender is unlikely to comply with probation orders and advises the court to that effect.

If probation is the sentence, the court often requires that the offender pay a fine or make restitution to victims, or perform community service work (usually on weekends). A rehabilitation plan might require various forms of counseling. It might forbid the offender from associating with specified friends or associates who, in the opinion of the court, could lead the offender astray—or who, on the other hand, might be victimized by the offender. The probation officer is responsible for seeing that the terms of release are met. If they aren't, the officer might recommend that probation be revoked and that the full sentence be imposed. Probation officers are sometimes called to deal with violations and other problems late at night and on weekends.

Since most of those on probation are young people or first-time offenders, many probation jobs deal with juveniles. Some youthful offenders are especially rebellious, arrogant, manipulative, and uncooperative.

Parole officers likewise work with offenders who have been released into society, but their cases are quite different from those usually assigned to probation workers. A large part of their contribution to society is to help veteran inmates adjust as they reenter the community. The parole period usually extends until the end of the prisoner's original sentence. For example, an offender may be sentenced to between two and six years in prison. At the end of three years, the parole board may grant a release. The prisoner is free but is under parole—held

Probation officers visit clients regularly to check on their progress and help solve problems. Many probation officers have heavy caseloads. They may be called out at odd hours.

accountable to the parole officer and to the terms of prerelease—for the remaining three years of the sentence. Hopefully, by that time, the offender will have become a law-abiding citizen who is contributing to society and will not return to crime.

To see that this happens, the parole officer tries to help the released offender find a meaningful job and, if necessary, a stable home. The parolee may need substance abuse counseling, job training, or psychiatric help. Periodically (several times per week or month, depending on the parole terms and on the officer's caseload), the officer and offender meet to discuss concerns. From time to time, the parole officer will confer with the client's relatives, acquaintances, and employer to stay apprised of the individual's progress.

Careful case notes are important here, as they are with probation clients. The parolee's performance during the release period must be reported periodically to the parole board.

Like probation officers, parole officers are sometimes assigned in advance to investigate a promising inmate's records and personal situation, such as home life and job prospects, and to advise the parole board whether or not an early release is wise. This investigation may include interviews with corrections officers and other prison employees to discuss the inmate's behavior.

Offenders who are out on probation have a strong incentive to comply with the terms, because if they don't, the court may order them to serve their full prison sentences. Offenders who violate parole know that if they're caught, they will be returned to confinement—likely with additional penalties for parole violation.

Too often, though, offenders who are free on probation or parole do not follow the rules. Some fail to report regularly and refuse to be held accountable. Some relocate to other cities or states and ignore their release terms altogether. And many resume criminal activities.

Some probation and parole officers are armed and authorized to apprehend violators. In most cases, though, they can't physically force their clients to obey court orders because the offenders are not confined and can leave the area. But if and when the violators are rearrested, the reports of their supervising corrections officials will have a considerable bearing on their future sentencing.

Perhaps the most difficult part of the probation or parole officer's job is the caseload. Most government agencies are stingy about hiring additional workers in the area of corrections; they do so only when necessary. Probation and parole officers thus find themselves overwhelmed with clients. This heavy caseload makes for long hours and impaired

Mixed Jobs

Many corrections job descriptions are combinations of multiple jobs. Some corrections officers ("guards"), for example, may be called on to supervise prisoner work and recreational activities, handle paperwork, provide instruction, and even perform a basic level of counseling. Intake officers at smaller institutions may spend much of their time doing administrative tasks that have little to do with processing paperwork for new inmates.

Multipurpose jobs can be either tedious or difficult to perform, especially when a corrections employee has to perform tasks that seem to have little or nothing, directly, to do with corrections. But they also can provide interesting challenges, and they can equip the worker with secondary skills that will lead to unexpected and exciting opportunities for advancement.

work quality because they cannot afford to spend too much time on any single case.

RESTORING INMATES TO VALUABLE ROLES

Inside the jail and prison setting, numerous professionals are at work for the benefit of the inmates. They include psychologists who deal with mental

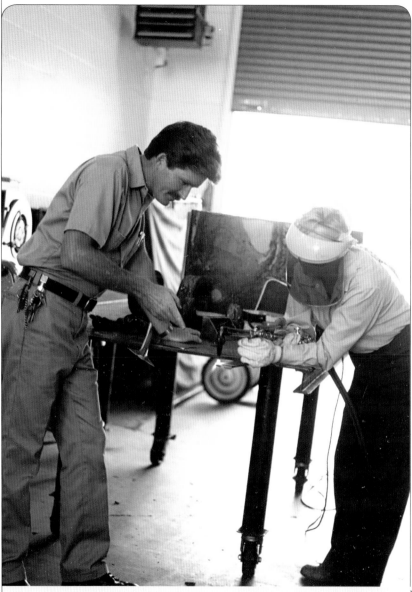

A prison instructor teaches an inmate welding at a Florida correctional institution. Providing prisoners with valuable job skills can help lead to productive, crime-free lives after they are released.

and emotional issues, vocational instructors who prepare inmates for jobs after their release, chaplains who see to prisoners' spiritual needs, administrators and clerical staff, transportation personnel, legal professionals, and many other specialists. Instructors teach educational and vocational classes and oversee prison jobs, such as making furniture, license plates, and other products; servicing computers and other types of equipment; and operating print shops. Some educational professionals are assigned to help inmates acquire high school diploma equivalents and to learn advanced skills in clerical subjects, electronics, and languages.

Caseworkers and counseling specialists are needed at all government correctional levels to work with inmates, especially those whose sentences are coming to an end. Caseworkers manage an offender's case from sentencing to release. Counselors with different qualifications deal with inmates in specific areas, such as substance abuse, family problems, and employment.

As they reenter society, inmates face special challenges brought about by their time in confinement and their criminal records. Some people—including close relatives—will treat them as outcasts, even after they have served their time. It may be harder for them than for other applicants to obtain jobs. While they enjoy a great sense of freedom upon release, they also face stresses in adjusting to a lifestyle that is very different from what they've experienced behind bars. Many released offenders are unable to cope and, all too soon, return to the corrections system. Trained counselors can help them make successful transitions back to society.

Counselors and caseworkers who work in the corrections field are hired by government agencies, corrections facilities, and courts. They meet with offenders, usually in their offices, to discuss and evaluate such matters as personal and family needs and problems, substance dependencies, job skills and employment training needs, and other concerns. Counselors in juvenile corrections programs strive to provide guidance that will break the young offender out of what could become a lifelong criminal cycle. Often, the counselor and caseworker function as members of a team that might also include substance abuse professionals, vocational instructors, family service workers, health specialists, and probation staff.

The caseworker and counselor must have good management skills. Their tasks range from record keeping to budget planning, and report writing to policy making.

Advancement opportunities for counselors and caseworkers are varied. Supervisory roles are most common—directors, managers, and coordinators of corrections-related services, including halfway houses. Some counselors decide to focus their careers in specific areas where they think they can have the greatest positive influence: helping teenage offenders, working with substance-dependent offenders, or providing educational and vocational advice.

Medical workers, too, are vital members of correctional teams today. In times past, prisoners in many facilities received no medical treatment aside from the basic first aid that corrections officers or other inmates could provide. Outside doctors

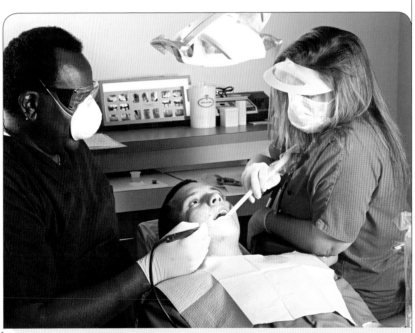

Correctional institutions are required to provide inmates with medical care—in this case, dental treatment. In the past, inmates suffered and sometimes died for lack of proper health care.

perhaps made periodic visits to examine inmates with severe conditions. Many prisoners languished and died of easily treatable medical problems.

Today, regular medical staff members attend to inmates' health issues. Some doctors, nurses, dentists, and other medical professionals find that administering their talents and using their knowledge inside jails and prisons is especially rewarding. Of particular concern are aging prisoners who develop debilitating and terminal illnesses, and who must continue to serve time despite their conditions. In some prisons, hospices that provide special care and privileges are available for those who are in their final months or years of life.

REINTRODUCING OFFENDERS TO SOCIETY

Halfway house staff must have many of the same skills as caseworkers and counselors. They work directly with offenders who have been released from prison but are not entirely free yet. Halfway houses are temporary supervised residences within the community for prisoners who are nearing the end of their terms. The transitioning individuals must conform to the rules of the halfway house and satisfy the conditions of their release, such as completion of substance abuse programs, job assignments, and vocational training. Residents of

At a halfway house in New Jersey, a teacher provides residents with instruction in cognitive skills. Such training teaches offenders to think through the results of a crime before committing it.

the halfway house must demonstrate that they, indeed, are ready to return to society.

The halfway house manager must also know how to operate a correctional residence and run a business. The job involves staff management, budgeting, security and safety matters, upkeep of the facility, and an unending flow of paperwork.

Applicants for all of these jobs should keep in mind that although they are not primarily responsible for security, they are working with lawbreakers—people who have had to be removed from society. Even for counselors, who generally work inside their offices, away from the cell blocks, tense situations can arise that call for quick thinking.

AT THE TOP OF THE PROFESSION

Prison administrators are usually the highest-paid corrections professionals. Consequently, they generally have higher levels of education and the broadest range of experience. Many have master's degrees; some hold doctorates.

Serving as the warden of a prison is considered the ultimate job in corrections. Although they may not have perpetual contact with the prison population, wardens are responsible for managing hundreds and, in some systems, thousands of corrections professionals—who, in turn, may be

Quala Champagne

Quala Champagne made history in 2003 when she was appointed warden of the Racine Correctional Institution in Wisconsin. Female wardens are a minority within the leadership of most corrections systems. Champagne was only the fifth woman—and the first African American woman—to head a major Wisconsin prison. The Racine prison is a medium-security institution for men.

She was well qualified for the job. At age thirty-seven, she had already worked in the state's corrections system for twelve years after obtaining a bachelor's degree in psychology and a master's degree in education. She began her career as a social worker at a juvenile correctional facility and served in several other roles, including deputy superintendent, there and at other institutions.

Champagne continues to advance in her corrections career. In 2005, she was appointed administrator of the Division of Community Corrections within the Wisconsin Department of Corrections.

Her motto in working with inmates is as follows: "Treat people humanely." When interviewed by the *Milwaukee Journal Sentinel* upon her appointment as warden, she commented, "I believe in giving individuals the opportunity to communicate."

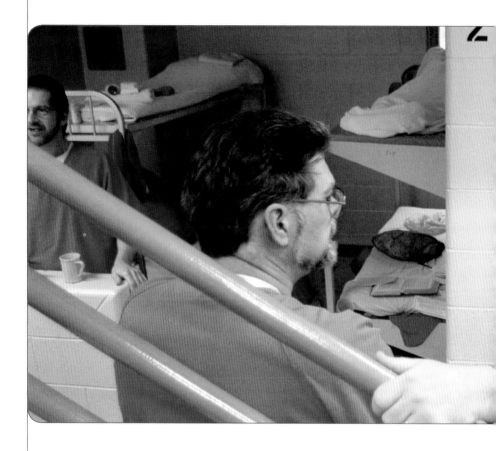

overseeing more than five thousand offenders. The warden must thoroughly understand every aspect of prison operations, from food service to staffing matters, because ultimately, the warden is responsible for all problems that arise.

The great majority of wardens today served as corrections officers early in their careers. Most have additional experience in counseling and administration. A prison warden must be educated not just in criminal justice but also in areas such as

In Bedford County, Pennsylvania, prison warden Brian Clark (*right*) talks with an inmate. Wardens must perform many tasks, but most make time to spend in direct contact with prisoners.

law, sociology, psychology, business administration, and political science. The warden wears many different hats. For instance, the individual must have excellent communication skills in order to meet the press effectively to discuss plans and to answer questions in controversial situations. The warden must manage the prison's budget; in large prison systems, the annual operating budget may be more than $100 million. In addition, the warden and other administrators are regularly engaged in planning and finding funds for new buildings and staff expansion.

Only a handful of corrections veterans can ever become wardens, not because they aren't qualified, but because the number of warden posts is limited to the number of correctional institutions.

Is there a next step up for prison wardens? Not many higher jobs exist in corrections. A few wardens are appointed to government criminal justice offices, chosen to oversee the whole system of corrections that operates under a government agency. Most, though, retire.

WHAT DO YOU NEED TO KNOW?

4

Just as the career opportunities in corrections are wide-ranging, so are educational and training requirements. Certain positions at some facilities call for few prior qualifications. Others require undergraduate and postgraduate college degrees, plus extensive experience.

At some state and local facilities, the only requirements for a prospective corrections officer are a high school education and special training that will be provided at the correctional facility. These jobs usually offer the low end of the salary range, and career advancement is likely to be slow.

Most corrections workers today have either college or technical school degrees. Many have advanced degrees.

TYPICAL COLLEGE MAJORS

Appropriate college majors for prospective corrections officers include criminal justice,

criminology, and police science. Other degrees that often lead to interesting corrections careers include sociology, social work, counseling, and psychology.

A college degree program will give the student a great breadth and depth of understanding about corrections and criminal justice systems. Courses available to criminal justice majors vary widely, from administration and economics to human behavior,

Students participate in a criminal justice class at St. Leo University in Florida. St. Leo University is one of many higher learning institutions that offer instruction in criminal justice.

pharmacology, safety and telecommunications. The student will also study a selected foreign language and take basic courses including science, history, and English.

The objective of a college curriculum is to teach the aspiring criminal justice professional not only about the judicial and legal systems but also about a variety of subjects that will have a bearing in the workplace. Obviously, a graduate of such a degree program will enter the corrections workforce with a far greater knowledge of the job than those with limited educations.

Probation and parole officers in most systems must have bachelor's degrees in majors such as social work or criminal justice. Some agencies require postgraduate education. Experience is not required in some settings, but others call for one or more years of work in a related field, such as casework, the supervision of criminal offenders, or criminal investigation. Applicants should be able to communicate effectively with offenders from all backgrounds. Fluency in a second language is a plus.

A corrections counselor will need education and experience in psychology (understanding the criminal mind and how to prevent recidivism [the relapse into criminal behavior]) and in working with individuals who have different types of personal problems—including substance dependence, uncontrollable anger, and various forms of psychological disorders. The counselor must know how to maintain an effective, safe counselor/client relationship with inmates. Some positions require past experience in conducting group counseling sessions.

For counseling specialists who are applying for federal corrections jobs, two years of graduate-level education in social or behavioral sciences is required, or a satisfactory combination of advanced study and experience.

Psychologists, doctors, nurses, and lawyers who commit to corrections-related careers must attain higher levels of education specific to their professions. Most psychologists in federal corrections systems hold doctoral degrees. They must diagnose and treat a variety of mental illnesses and emotional and personality disorders among prisoners. They also support the corrections staff, providing crisis and stress counseling, and helping to negotiate hostage situations and other conflicts. Besides their academic degrees, they must undergo corrections training at the Bureau of Prisons' academy in Glynco, Georgia.

Correctional facilities also employ clerical, maintenance, and other workers whose jobs require appropriate qualifications and training. Some corrections jobs call for weapons and self-defense expertise. In other roles, it is unnecessary.

Although a bachelor's degree might not be required to obtain an exciting and rewarding job, young people interested in this career field should keep in mind the future. A higher educational level improves the likelihood of advancement to better jobs, and it's generally easier to obtain a college degree earlier in life than later. The worker who has earned a degree will likely receive quicker promotions and find a greater variety of job

Newly hired federal corrections officers and other prison personnel must undergo extensive training at a Bureau of Prisons' training center in Glynco, Georgia.

openings available. If a special area of corrections is of interest, additional education and training in that particular category will greatly improve job advancement potential.

There is an additional incentive for a prospective corrections worker to obtain an advanced degree or certificate: It tells the employer that the applicant is serious about a corrections career—serious enough to invest substantial time and money

acquiring a suitable degree before even attempting to enter the job market.

BEYOND BOOK KNOWLEDGE

Besides their knowledge of the corrections process, law, and human behavior, corrections officers will learn from experience. They must understand the laws that apply in the prison and jail environment.

They need to become thoroughly familiar with the policies of the institution where they work. They must be able to perceive personal traits and mannerisms of prisoners that might suggest trouble. For example, they must learn to recognize symptoms of substance use and subtle animosity that might exist between inmates. They also need to be sensitive to social issues, such as cultural and racial diversity. They must learn basic emergency response techniques—first aid, cardiopulmonary resuscitation (CPR), and firefighting, for example.

They must also possess certain essential personal traits. These include the ability to respond appropriately and quickly in potentially dangerous situations, the ability to keep a cool head and calm outward attitude, and good organizational skills.

Corrections officers and workers in certain other areas of the corrections system will undergo training much like that of police officers. They must learn self-defense tactics and the use of different kinds of weapons. Naturally, they must stay in good physical condition.

Most bailiff positions require only a high school diploma or GED, unless the bailiff is a regular law enforcement officer, in which case the agency's normal educational requirements apply. Much of the bailiff's training—learning courtroom practices, terms, and special security needs inside a

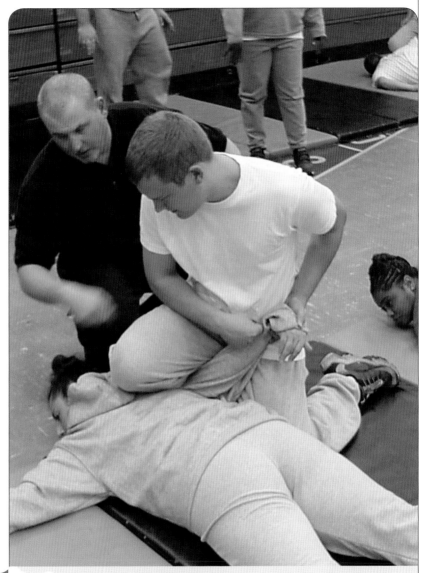

Some corrections professionals must be skilled in self-defense techniques. Here, trainees learn to immobilize suspects at an academy in Michigan.

courthouse—is provided on the job by the court and/or the sponsoring law enforcement agency.

"EXPERIENCE REQUIRED"?

Entry-level positions usually provide on-the-job training for new employees. In some cases, the training may be as brief as a few weeks or months. In others, it may continue for a year or longer. Some corrections personnel are required to take additional training from time to time, such as instruction in using new firearms and mastering new prison procedures.

Many corrections jobs, however, require applicants to already have experience in the job-related field—administration, security, counseling or casework, or substance abuse or probation programs, for example. It is essential that correctional facilities be operated by experienced staff. Some will not hire and train applicants who have completed their education but lack experience.

How can a newcomer get a job with no experience, and how can the applicant obtain experience if he or she is unable to get a job? Although it's a difficult dilemma in some situations, there are solutions. Aspiring corrections workers may have to begin by obtaining jobs in related fields in order to acquire experience before they qualify for the jobs they really want. They might find work as night guards at a factory site, for instance, or as security officers at a retail mall. However, they might already possess helpful experience they don't realize they have. Previous employment in outside fields might have equipped them with advanced communication and problem-solving skills, the ability to manage several tasks simultaneously, an understanding of efficient record-keeping and case or project management software, experience supervising other workers, and experience handling crises. When applying, they should point out any special qualifications that may be useful, even if their previous jobs had nothing to do with corrections.

Some corrections agencies, for certain job openings, allow advanced educational achievements to substitute for career experience, and vice versa. An inexperienced applicant who holds a master's degree or a second bachelor's degree or certificate in a related subject may be worth special consideration. The same might apply to a candidate who is fluent in two or more languages. This multilingual ability is of increasing value because the U.S. prison population consists of a growing number of Spanish-speaking inmates whose English skills are limited.

Computer and/or audio-visual expertise might also be a plus when applying for certain corrections jobs.

Applicants hired for federal prison jobs must undergo 120 hours of training at a Federal Bureau of Prisons facility in Georgia. Within their first year of employment, they must complete a total of 200 training hours. Training guidelines were created by the American Correctional Association and the American Jail Association.

Many young people who are interested in criminal justice careers obtain experience as security guards at shopping malls and other locations before seeking employment as corrections officers.

In many corrections jobs, rookie employees are assigned to work with veterans for the first few weeks or months.

Smart corrections workers keep in mind the adage that "education never ends." If they've never acquired an advanced degree, many dedicated corrections professionals enroll in part-time or

An Alternate Training Path: Military Service

Some of the standard education and training requirements are waived for job applicants who have served in the armed forces as corrections or security specialists. These individuals have already been trained in the handling of criminals, in the law, in self-defense and the use of weapons, and in other relevant subjects. Military containment facilities, just like civilian jails and prisons, require individuals with a wide variety of skills and knowledge, not merely security officers. Corrections administrators, counselors, and medical professionals are serving in different military branches, and many of them will seek related careers after they are discharged. They will enter the civilian job market with advanced qualifications and on-the-job experience.

High school students interested in the corrections field might want to consider a preliminary stint in a regular or reserve branch of the military, especially if money for college is a problem. Not only can they obtain free training and invaluable experience, but they can also use their military financial benefits later to pay for their further education.

night courses at nearby colleges or technical schools to earn corrections-related degrees or certificates. If they already have a higher-education degree, they take additional courses, perhaps with the goal of eventually obtaining a master's degree or a second bachelor's degree in a related study major that will give them special qualifications. Hundreds of colleges are offering more and more courses and even complete degree curricula online, making it convenient for adults to pursue higher education while working full-time.

Continuing education is one key to fast advancement in most careers, including corrections. A nice benefit is that many institutions pay some or all of their employees' tuition.

5

FINDING THE CORRECTIONS JOB FOR YOU

Almost all corrections jobs are funded by local, state, or federal governments. Most are at state-run prisons, low-security detention centers, or juvenile institutions. Interestingly, although state facilities and programs post more job openings, they typically pay less than either federal prison systems or city and county jails.

The Bureau of Labor Statistics' *Occupational Outlook Handbook, 2008–09 Edition*, describes corrections jobs in two categories: "correctional officers" and "probational officers and correctional treatment specialists." In both of those general employment fields, the prospects are bright. The handbook states that for corrections officers, "job opportunities are expected to be excellent." In fact, by 2012, the number of corrections officer jobs in the United States may increase by as much as 35 percent, as new facilities are opened and current employees retire or move to other jobs. For probation officers and treatment specialists, employment growth is expected to be "as fast as the average," although it largely "depends on government funding."

Sounds good, but how do job seekers find the jobs that most interest them?

Corrections-related job services are available online. One is the job search section of the Corrections Connection Web site (http://www. corrections.com/jobs/search). Visitors to the site can search, state-by-state, under some forty job titles. A few examples of the career possibilities include the following: caseworker, classification officer, clergy, community outreach counselor, computer/ information systems, corrections officer (two levels), education/teaching, finance, food service, graphic design, juvenile, K-9 (dog) officer, law, librarian, maintenance, medical, probation/parole officer, public information, and social services.

For young people who are interested in pursuing a federal career in corrections, a good place for initial research is the "Federal Prison Facilities" section of the Federal Bureau of Prisons (BOP) Web site (http://www.bop.gov/locations/index.jsp). There, they can locate every facility maintained by the Bureau of Prisons by state, region, or type of institution. They can find its location on a map and learn its security level, physical and mailing addresses, and visiting hours. Each week, the BOP publishes an itemized inmate population report. Besides its minimum-,

The Federal Bureau of Prisons' Web site (http://www.bop.gov) posts information about all its institutions around the country. It also offers career information for students and older job seekers.

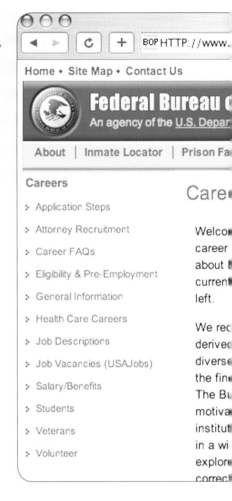

low-, medium-, and high-security prisons, the bureau provides information on its network of community corrections (residential reentry) centers.

To apply for a job at a federal correctional facility, go to the separate Bureau of Prisons Web page (http://www.bop.gov/recruit.html) and download the appropriate application form.

Federal Bureau of Prisons

index.jsp   Q▾ Google

Search [ ]   Website ⬍   Go

ers | Inmate Matters | Policy/Forms | Doing Business | News/Information

The Bureau of Prisons

ral Bureau of Prisons' (BOP)
web pages, where you can learn
the employment process, and
using the links provided to the

e Bureau's real strength is
f. The BOP "family" is a
and career-oriented team with
professionals in the country.
oximately 35,000 highly-
working in 114 correctional
e country [Locate a Facility] and
cupations. We encourage you to
es and consider a career in
Federal Bureau of Prisons

NEXT TESTIMONIAL ➡

Lamont Easter, Management Analyst

Other online services that can help locate corrections jobs include the Discover computerized career guidance program (http://www.act.org/discover). Structured particularly for young people, Discover helps students not only explore career fields but also identify an appropriate college. Job searchers might try popular services including

CareerBuilder (http://www.careerbuilder.com) and Monster (http://www.monster.com).

Persons who want to work in a specific correctional facility should go to its Web site (which might be found under the umbrella site of a city, county, state, or federal government agency). A simple word search should locate it. Searchers who want to work in a particular city or state can easily identify the correctional facilities in those locations. Usually, an institution's Web site will provide instructions for submitting job applications. Some organizations post descriptions of open jobs online. Otherwise, the candidate will have to submit an application to the facility or to the government agency in charge of it . . . and wait.

Meanwhile, don't overlook newspaper want ads. Different government agencies often post new job listings there. Local unemployment offices sometimes have information about corrections-related job openings.

APPLICATIONS AND INTERVIEWS

The applicant almost invariably will need to be a U.S. citizen who is at least eighteen years old (twenty-one, for some jobs). Job applicants in most fields are subject to background checks. Prospective employers will want to verify the person's education and employment history and learn about possible

Tips for Job Seekers

Begin by talking to corrections professionals. After hearing their experiences, the aspiring employee might decide the job would be a mistake or might foresee shortcomings in meeting the requirements.

Prepare for the job interview. The interviewer needs to know that the applicant has researched the job, understands (basically, at the very least) what it involves, has found out a good deal about the particular correctional institution or program setting, and understands the job requirements.

Don't be even one minute late for the scheduled interview. (But don't be obnoxiously early, either. An applicant should try to time arrival for the job interview about five to ten minutes before the appointment.)

Dress conservatively. People who operate correctional facilities are generally conservative. They have to be, in order to maintain an authoritative posture over wrongdoers who have nothing better to do than test the limits of what they can get away with. Regardless of stereotyping, if a corrections applicant arrives at a job interview looking more like a possible wrongdoer than like a disciplinarian, the applicant should not expect to be hired there anytime soon.

Express enthusiasm for the job. If the applicant is sure of a corrections career plan, the conviction should be obvious.

A standard interview question is, "Why do you want to work here?" The applicant must be able to answer it precisely, not in vague terms. ("I just wanna be a prison guard, and this looks like it might be a nice place to start.") The job seeker should emphasize an interest in the particular job and facility.

firings, criminal charges, and workers' compensation claims. Employers commonly ask for character references.

The corrections applicant may face even closer scrutiny. Obviously, the applicant must have no felony record or problematic job history. A drug test almost certainly will be required, and a polygraph (lie detector) test might be administered. Background checks for certain corrections jobs

When meeting with an employer or hiring specialist, it's important for the job seeker to make a good impression in person as well as on paper.

might include a review of driving records and credit reports as well.

If basically qualified for a job, an applicant hopefully will be called for an initial interview. Further interviews may be part of the hiring process. The candidate also will be given a series of tests that might include a federal civil service test and a psychological test, depending on the nature of the job. The successful candidate might be hired almost immediately or might face a follow-up process that could take weeks or months.

Remember that when a job hopeful applies to a government agency or to a correctional institution, the application might be placed on file indefinitely. It could be weeks, months, or even years before the application rises to the attention of the hiring official for an appropriate job that becomes open. Applicants who seriously want to work for a particular corrections facility should periodically send their updated résumés to the hiring office.

New employees in corrections, as in most careers, work under probationary status for at least ninety days. Basically, that means they are in a trial period; they are not considered permanent employees until they've proved they can handle the job. Trainees do not enjoy all the benefits of veteran employees. Their supervisors can dismiss them without having to document the reasons for dismissal, and the trainees might not be eligible yet to begin acquiring paid vacation time.

A WIDE RANGE OF SALARIES AND BENEFITS

A fairly brief online job search will reveal a striking range of salaries in corrections jobs. The state or geographic region has much to do with pay scales at corrections facilities. A worker in one state might be paid as much as twice the salary of a worker performing basically the same job in another state. The main reason is that state and local governments provide funding for most institutions, and some governing bodies are more willing than others to apply tax dollars to corrections systems.

In general, federal jobs pay more. Local (city and county) institutions are next in pay, while state institutions pay the lowest. Federal jobs, although perhaps more desirable, are harder to obtain. Fewer than 5 percent of corrections jobs in the United States come under federal authority. And since most federal systems are flooded with job applications, their hiring officials can be very selective, choosing only the best qualified candidates.

For counselors and caseworkers, the pay is typically about 20 percent higher than for corrections officers. (These roles usually require higher levels of education, too.) Corrections officers generally are paid slightly more for working night shifts and as much as 25 percent more for Sunday hours.

Wardens can earn six-figure salaries at large institutions in some states.

Job benefits for corrections workers in most situations are good to excellent. They may include full medical insurance, as well as personal leave days and substantial retirement pay. In federal jobs, corrections employees can retire after twenty-five years (or after twenty years, once they reach the age of fifty). Many corrections workers retire in

Three training lieutenants await students at the State Police Academy in Lansing, Michigan. Corrections officers and other correctional workers must be well prepared before they can perform effectively.

their late forties or early fifties and pursue second careers, while beginning to receive retirement benefits from their corrections service.

Most agencies furnish their officers with all the necessary equipment and uniforms or provide an expense allowance.

Regardless of the pay and benefits, a dedicated corrections worker is on the job to help improve the lives of those inside and outside the system— that is, to work toward a better society.

CHANGES, CHALLENGES, AND NEW CAREER OPPORTUNITIES

6

Corrections systems have been undergoing reforms and other changes for more than a century. Long gone are the days of galley slaves and chain gangs laboring mercilessly at the tips of overseers' whips. Convicted felons are no longer sentenced to transportation to Devil's Island, Tasmania, and other distant penal colonies where meager servings of stale bread and water once or twice a day were the only nourishment. Modern-day offenders, by contrast, receive decent meals, health care, exercise, counseling, and vocational training to prepare them for a new life after they have served their time. In lower-security facilities, they enjoy small luxuries in their cells, such as TVs, libraries, musical instruments, and computer access.

As prison life has changed, so has the definition of the corrections worker. Once, a stern, brutish, shotgun-wielding presence capable of maintaining authority was the

primary job qualification. Now, physical control is maintained for the most part with innovative technology: electric fences, computer-activated cell doors, coded electronic access to high-security areas, surveillance cameras, and microphones. As a last resort in violent conflicts, tactical response teams are equipped with state-of-the-art weapons and protection. As a result, the job description of today's corrections worker bears little resemblance

A guard monitors inmate activity via a bank of security screens inside the Juvenile Hall Annex in Santa Ana, California. Technology makes it easier—and safer—for correctional workers to do their jobs.

to that of a prison guard half a century ago. During that time, scores of new corrections careers— unheard of not so long ago—have been created.

UNDERSTAND THE SYSTEM

Before committing to a career in corrections, a young person should learn how the corrections system works, the different factors and forces that

What If Crime Declines?

The remarkable growth in the corrections career field has been fueled by the disturbing growth in the criminal offender population. The more inmates there are, the more corrections staff members are required to supervise and counsel them. While corrections professionals work to improve the prison system and to reduce the rate of recidivism, others in many career fields, from criminal justice to social sciences, are striving to lower crime rates and reduce prison populations.

By all indications, the upward trend in prison populations and corrections jobs isn't likely to change soon. In the event of significant crime reduction, though, corrections employment opportunities will diminish.

determine its operation, and changes that are affecting both inmates and corrections staff. Administrators face challenges not just in over-crowding and legal and ethical issues, but also in finding the money they need for their institutions to operate effectively. The budgets they forge will affect hiring, employee salaries, and advancement prospects. Job seekers entering this field should be aware not only of the tension inside a corrections compound, but also of the higher tension that affects the overall status of the facility where they will work (and its employees).

Money is arguably the greatest difficulty facing correctional facility administrators. They receive funds from taxes. In order to get what they believe is their fair share of tax dollars, they must persuade elected politicians to support the corrections system. Many taxpayers—the people who elect and oust politicians—complain that they already are paying too much for lawbreakers to be "pampered." They don't want to see more of their tax money go to correctional institutions or to probation and counseling programs.

Like it or not, city, county, state, and federal governments are required to accommodate growing inmate populations. All predictions are that corrections will continue to be a dynamic, promising career field, not only for security officers but also for professionals with a diverse range of interests, skills, and education. But it is unlikely to be a path to wealth. The salaries of government employees are determined by how tax revenues are distributed to different agencies. In the end, they depend on the willingness of taxpayers to support the corrections system.

Corrections employees in all roles are working with individuals convicted of crimes. They live in an environment filled with many negative elements: fear, suspicion, uncertainty, low self-esteem, emotional

An officer patrols a cell block during a lockdown at California State Prison, Sacramento. Although the scene appears lonely, prisons are tense places, especially during lockdowns, when all inmates are confined to their cells.

manipulation, bitterness, resentment, and anger. Many inmates are people who simply made a serious mistake and are paying for it. They are well-behaved, hoping to complete their sentences without problems and return to a regular life. Others have psychological and behavioral characteristics that translate into violence. But they all have certain things in common, including rights that must be protected.

Corrections workers are constantly mindful of the hazards that surround them. At the same time, they know that by treating offenders with respect and performing their jobs effectively, they can make a positive difference in society.

GLOSSARY

amnesty Forgiveness of a prosecutable offense.

arsenal A collection of weapons.

contraband Forbidden items inside a prison, including drugs, weapons, and objects from which weapons can be made.

detention centers Correctional facilities designed to house special categories of inmates, such as juveniles.

felony A serious crime punishable by imprisonment.

forfeiture The surrender of property as part of the punishment for a crime. Examples of confiscated items include weapons and vehicles that were used for transporting drugs or stolen goods.

GED General equivalency diploma (substitute for a high school diploma).

incarceration Confinement in a correctional facility.

itinerant Traveling from place to place.

jurisdiction A category or geographic area of court or law enforcement authority.

marksmanship Exceptional skill with firearms.

misdemeanor A minor offense usually punishable by a fine, probation, or community service term.

parole Early release from prison under supervised
    monitoring.
probation Suspension of a prison sentence or fine
    under the condition that the offender obey
    supervisory rules.
recidivism A former prisoner's eventual return to
    criminal behavior after release.
rehabilitation The process of restoring an offender
    to a useful, law-abiding role in society.
restitution A court order for a thief or vandal to
    return stolen property or pay a victim the value
    of stolen or damaged property.
sentry An armed lookout, such as a sharpshooter
    in a tower overlooking prison grounds.
warden Director of a prison.

FOR MORE INFORMATION

American Correctional Association
206 North Washington Street
Alexandria, VA 22314
(800) ACA-JOIN (222-5646)
Web site: http://www.aca.org
This is the world's oldest and largest international correctional association. It is involved with all areas of corrections.

American Jail Association
1135 Professional Court
Hagerstown, MD 21740-5853
(301) 790-3930
Web site: http://www.aja.org
The American Jail Association is a national, nonprofit support group for jail operators that "focuses exclusively on issues specific to the operations of local correctional facilities."

American Probation and Parole Association
2760 Research Park Drive
Lexington, KY 40511-8410
(859) 244-8203

Web site: http://www.appa-net.org
This association provides information, training, and
assistance in the field of community-based corrections.

Association of Halfway House
Alcoholism Programs

401 East Sangamon Avenue
Springfield, IL 62702
(217) 523-0527
Web site: http://www.ahhap.org
This organization promotes the quality operation of
halfway houses, sober living residences, transitional
living facilities, and other community facilities for those
with alcohol problems.

Bureau of Justice Statistics

U.S. Department of Justice
810 Seventh Street NW
Washington, DC 20531
(202) 307-0765
Web site: http://www.ojp.usdoj.gov/bjs
The bureau publishes information on crime, criminals,
victims, and justice systems.

Bureau of Prisons

U.S. Department of Justice
320 First Street NW
Washington, DC 20534
Web site: http://bop.gov

The Bureau of Prisons' mission is to protect society "by confining offenders in the controlled environments of prisons and community-based facilities that are safe, humane, cost-efficient, and appropriately secure, and that provide work and other self-improvement opportunities to assist offenders in becoming law-abiding citizens." See especially http://bop.gov/recruit.html.

Correctional Service of Canada
340 Laurier Avenue W
Ottawa, ON K1A 0O9
Canada
(913) 922-5891
Web site: http://www.csc-scc.gc.ca
This Canadian federal government agency is responsible for administering sentences of two years or longer.

Council of Juvenile Correctional Administrators
170 Forbes Road, Suite 106
Braintree, MA 02184
(781) 843-2663
Web site: http://cjca.net/default.aspx
A nonprofit organization, this council is dedicated to improving local juvenile corrections programs and services.

National Commission on Correctional Health Care
1145 West Diversey Parkway
Chicago, IL 60614

(773) 880-1460
Web site: http://www.ncchc.org
This commission is dedicated to improving the quality
of health care in prisons, jails, and juvenile confinement
institutions.

National Parole Board
Ministry of Public Safety Canada
410 Laurier Avenue W
Ottawa, ON K1A 0R1
Canada
(613) 954-7474
Web site: http://www.npb-cnic.gc.ca
The National Parole Board has the authority under
Canada's Corrections and Conditional Release Act to
grant and revoke paroles.

WEB SITES

Due to the changing nature of Internet links,
Rosen Publishing has developed an online list of
Web sites related to the subject of this book. This
site is updated regularly. Please use this link to
access the list:

http://www.rosenlinks.com/ccj/corr

FOR FURTHER READING

Ackerman, Thomas H. *Federal Law Enforcement Careers: Profiles of 250 High-Powered Positions and Surefire Tactics for Getting Hired.* 2nd ed. Indianapolis, IN: JIST Publishing, Inc., 2006.

Baxter, Neale J. *Opportunities in Government Careers.* Columbus, OH: McGraw-Hill, 2001.

Bolles, Richard Nelson, et al. *What Color Is Your Parachute? For Teens: Discovering Yourself, Defining Your Future.* Berkeley, CA: Ten Speed Press, 2006.

Clinton, Susan. *Correction Officer* (Careers Without College). Mankato, MN: Capstone Press, 1998.

Corrections Officer Exam. New York, NY: Learning Express, 2007.

Harr, J. Scott, and Karen M. Hess. *Careers in Criminal Justice and Related Fields: From Internship to Promotion.* 5th ed. Belmont, CA: Wadsworth Publishing, 2006.

Reeves, Diane Lindsey, and Gail Karlitz. *Career Ideas for Teens in Law and Public Safety.* New York, NY: Checkmark Books, 2006.

Schroeder, Donald, and Frank Lombardo. *Barron's Correction Officer Exam.* 3rd ed. Hauppauge, NY: Barron's Educational Series, Inc., 2008.

Weiss, Jodi, and Russell Kahn. *145 Things to Be When You Grow Up* (Career Guides). New York, NY: Princeton Review, 2004.

BIBLIOGRAPHY

Ackerman, Thomas H. *Federal Law Enforcement Careers: Profiles of 250 High-Powered Positions and Surefire Tactics for Getting Hired*. 2nd ed. Indianapolis, IN: JIST Publishing, Inc., 2006.

Bagley, Paul D. *The Everything Guide to Careers in Law Enforcement*. Avon, MA: Adams Media, 2007.

California Department of Corrections and Rehabilitation. Departmental Web site. Retrieved September 11, 2008 (http://www.cdcr.ca.gov).

"Correctional Officers." *Occupational Outlook Handbook, 2008–09 Edition*. Bureau of Labor Statistics, U.S. Department of Labor. Retrieved September 11, 2008 (http://www.bls.gov/oco/ocos156.htm).

Echaore-McDavid, Susan. *Law Enforcement, Security, and Protective Services*. 2nd ed. New York, NY: Checkmark Books, 2006.

"Frank Appoints Quala Champagne as New DCC Administrator." Wisconsin Department of Corrections News Release, October 18, 2005. Retrieved September 13, 2008 (http://www.wi-doc.com/Champagne_DCC.htm).

Herman, Peter G., editor. *The American Prison System* (The Reference Shelf). Bronx, NY: The H. W. Wilson Company, 2001.

Lambert, Stephen, and Debra Regan. *Great Jobs for Criminal Justice Majors*. Chicago, IL: VGM Career Books, 2001.

Missouri Department of Corrections. Departmental Web site. Retrieved September 11, 2008 (http://www.doc.missouri.gov).

North Carolina Department of Corrections. Departmental Web site. Retrieved September 11, 2008 (http://www.doc.state.nc.us).

"One in Every 31 U.S. Adults Was in a Prison or Jail or on Probation or Parole at the End of Last Year." U.S. Department of Justice press release, December 5, 2007. Retrieved September 11, 2008 (http://www.corrections.com/links/link/240).

"Prisoners in 2006." U.S. Department of Justice, Bureau of Justice Statistics. Retrieved September 11, 2008 (http://www.corrections.com/links/link/240).

"Probation Officers and Correctional Treatment Specialists." *Occupational Outlook Handbook, 2008–09 Edition*. Bureau of Labor Statistics, U.S. Department of Labor. Retrieved September 11, 2008 (http://www.bls.gov/oco/ocos265.htm).

Provorse, Jane. "Quala Champagne: Wisconsin's First Black Woman Warden." *Alumni &*

Friends, University of Wisconsin-Whitewater, Winter/Spring 2004. Retrieved September 13, 2008 (http://www.uww.edu/cls/success/alumni/champagne_quala.html).

Roth, Mitchel P. *Prisons and Prison Systems: A Global Encyclopedia*. Westport, CT: Greenwood Press, 2006.

Sykes, Leonard, Jr. "Hoping to Make Her Mark: First African-American Woman to Head State Prison." *Milwaukee Journal Sentinel*, August 31, 2003. Retrieved September 13, 2008 (http://www.jsonline.com/story/index.aspx?id=166216).

INDEX

ABOUT THE AUTHOR

Daniel E. Harmon is the author of more than sixty books and numerous articles for national and regional magazines and newspapers. *Careers in Explosives and Arson Investigation*, his book for Rosen Publishing's Careers in Forensics series, was published in 2008. He has also written educational books about the Federal Bureau of Investigation, the U.S. Attorney General's Office, the armed forces, the U.S. Food and Drug Administration, the Environmental Protection Agency, psychological disorders, and the role of defense lawyers. He lives in Spartanburg, South Carolina.

PHOTO CREDITS

Cover, p. 1 © www.istockphoto.com/Jacom Stephens; cover (background) © www.istockphoto.com/Steven Robert; cover (bottom) © www.istockphoto.com/Joerg Reiman; cover (back) © www.istockphoto.com/Jesse Karjalai; pp. 5, 13, 50, 57 © Jonathan Allain; pp. 10–11 California Department of Corrections and Rehabilitation; p. 15 © Damian Dovarganes/ AFP Getty Images; pp. 19, 20, 22–23, 30–31, 38, 42, 62–63, 66–67, 96 © AP Images; p. 28 © Melanie Stetson Freeman/ *Christian Science Monitor* via Getty Images; p. 35 © David R. Frazier/The Image Works; pp. 46–47 © Reprinted with permission of the American Correctional Association, Alexandria, Virginia; pp. 54, 70–71 Federal Bureau of Prisons; p. 59 © KRT Photos/Newscom; pp. 73, 90 Michigan Department of Corrections; pp. 76–77 © Mario Tama/Getty Images; pp. 86–87 © Kayte M. Deioma; pp. 92–93 © Spencer Grant/Photo Edit; back cover © www.istockphoto.com/ Jesse Karjalai.

Designer: Les Kanturek; Editor: Kathy Kuhtz Campbell
Photo Researcher: Marty Levick